Dear Parents/Teachers:

Yay! Your child/student is interest in learning to read!
The goal: reading on their own and loving it!

Waldorf Readers are designed to help your child/student enjoy the learning process. Our Readers have 4 levels to guide your child/student to independent reading.

Each level collection has interesting stories, unique characters and colorful illustrations. All Waldorf Readers are original works with characters your child/student will enjoy. Waldorf Publishing strives to accommodate a full reading experience for any child/student at any reading level.

Waldorf Readers will entertain your child/student level by level.

Spark Reading   **Preschool-Kindergarten**
-Large font and easy words
-Illustrations to accompany the storyline
-No more than two syllables

Level 1 Waldorf Readers introduce children/students to reading. Sentences are short and simple. Using phonics skills, children/students will sound out words.

Read Together   **Preschool-Grade 1**
-Short sentences
-Easy to understand stories
-Simple vocabulary
-No more than two syllables

Level 2 Waldorf Readers keep the excitement for reading strong. Sentences will include bigger words and more in depth story lines, which are sure to entertain.

Independent Reading   **Grade 1-3**
-Exciting and relatable characters
-Plots and story lines that are relatable and easy to follow
-Topics children enjoy
-No more than 3 syllable words

Level 3 Waldorf Readers have larger paragraphs and words that will challenge and engage children/students.

Advanced Independent Reading   **Grade 2-4**
-In depth plot and story lines
-Larger blocks of text
-Full color illustration
-Words with 3+ syllables

Level 4 Waldorf Readers are more challenging and lengthy. These books are perfect for children/students who want to read longer books and still enjoy colorful illustrations. Level 4 Waldorf Readers are the last level before advancing to Waldorf Chapter Books.

Published by Waldorf Publishing
2140 Hall Johnson Road
#102-345
Grapevine, Texas 76051
www.WaldorfPublishing.com

What are Microscopes?

ISBN: 9781647648978

Library of Congress Control Number: 2020932749

Copyright © 2020

All rights reserved. No part of this book may be reproduced or transmitted in any form or by any means whatsoever without express written permission from the author, except in the case of brief quotations embodied in critical articles and reviews. Please refer all pertinent questions to the publisher. All rights reserved. No part of this book may be reproduced or transmitted in any form or by any means, electronic or mechanical, including photocopying, recording, or by an information storage and retrieval system except by a reviewer who may quote brief passages in a review to be printed in a magazine or newspaper without permission in writing from the publisher.

Illustrations by Ksennia Kudriavtseva
Design by Baris Celik

What are Microscopes?

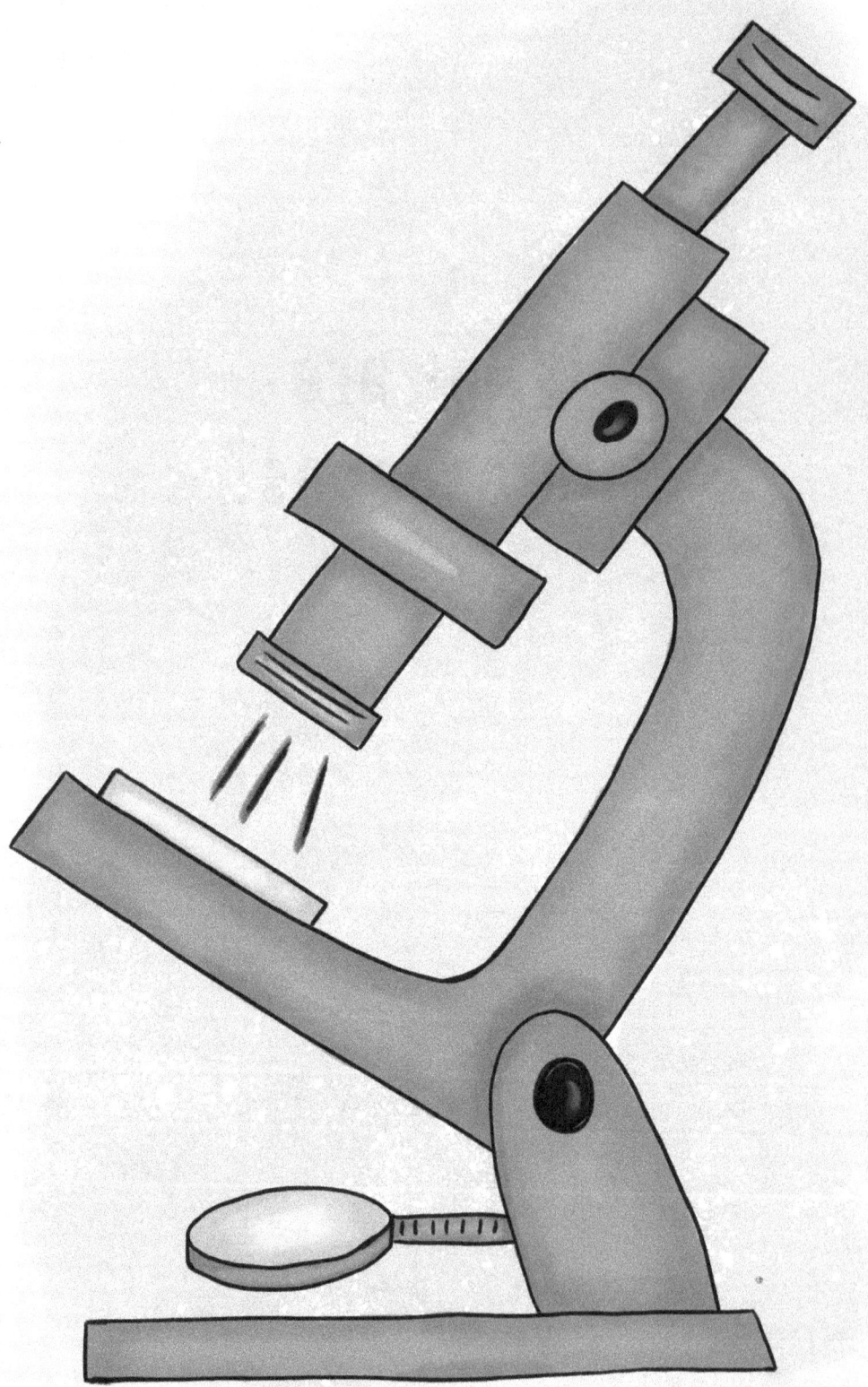

Have you ever heard of a microscope?

Well, I don't mean to brag, but that's partly my invention! Let me introduce myself. I'm Antonie Phillips van Leeuwenhoek (my last name is pronounced "von lee ooh wen huke"). Now try saying that ten times fast!

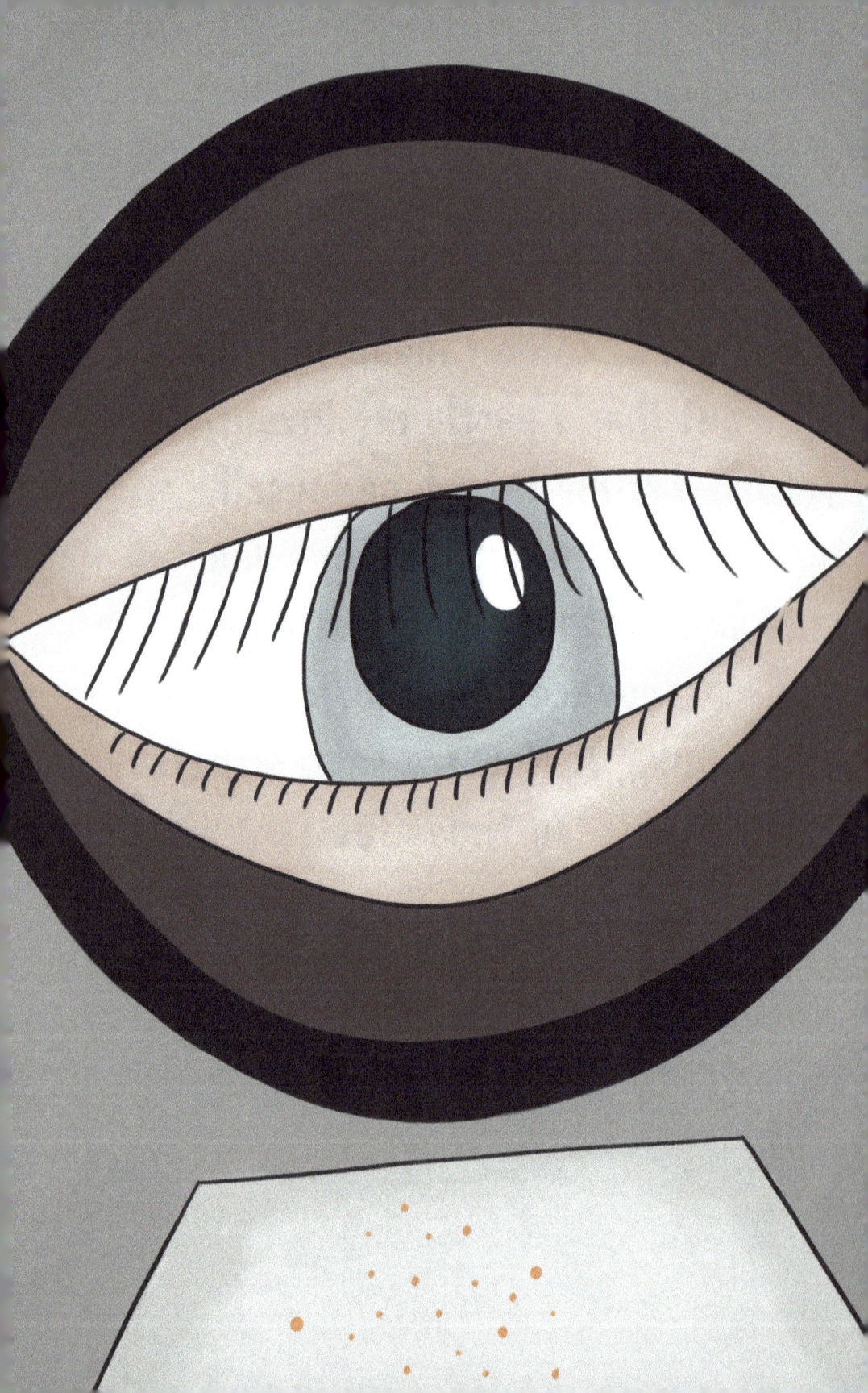

For those of you who don't know, a microscope is a tool that scientists use to study objects that are too small to be seen by the naked eye. Is that cool, or what?

Oh, in case you don't already know this either, a scientist is a person who studies something he is curious about, such as nature, to help the world understand more about it.

But people that aren't scientists, like kids, can use microscopes too!
So don't feel left out!

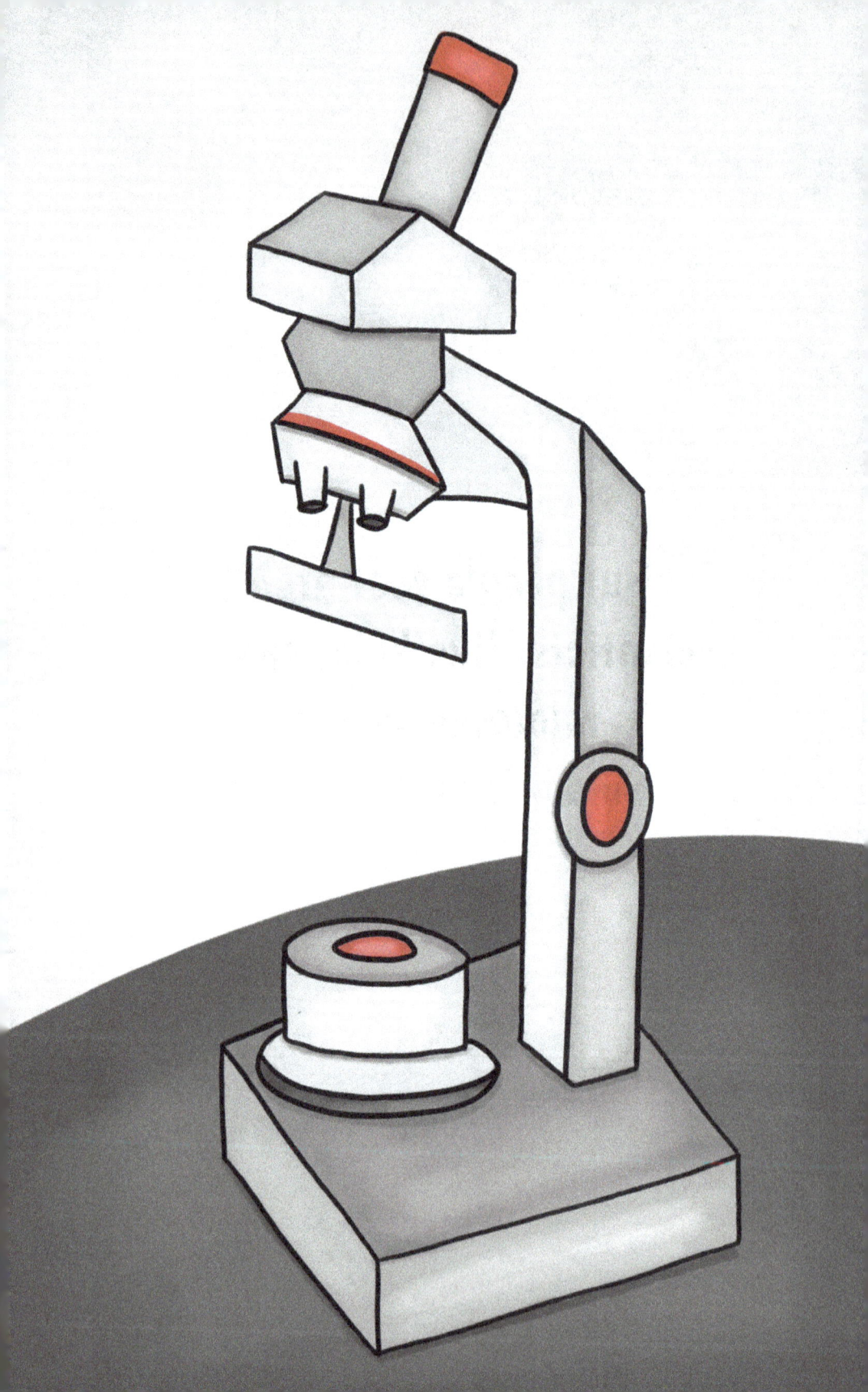

There are many types of microscopes. Light microscopes can be used right in your home or school to view very cool, tiny things.

So, in addition to helping to invent the microscope, I was also one of the first scientists to use one.

I was born a very long time ago, on October 24, 1632.

My homeland was Holland, which is a country in Europe.

So, if we do the math, that means I was born almost 400 years ago!

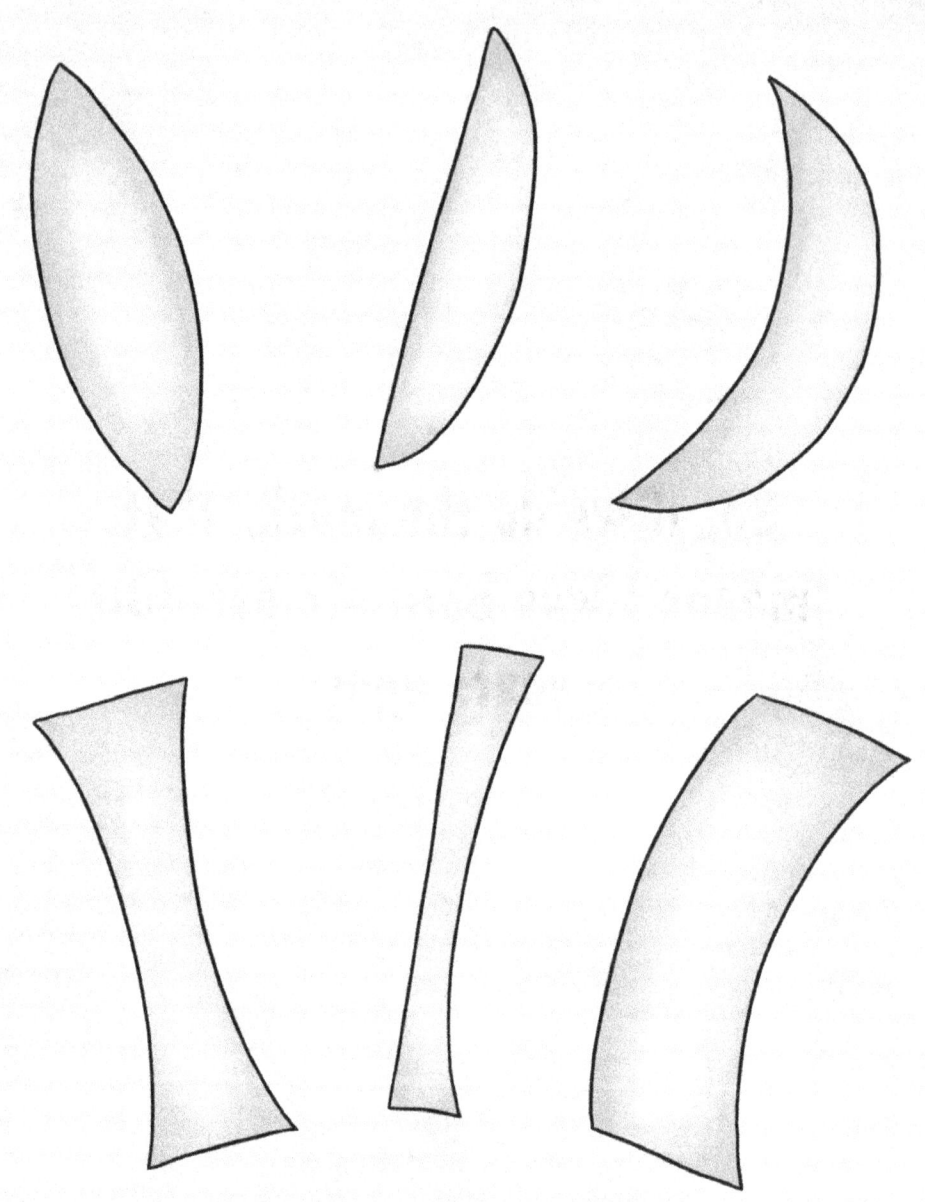

Again, I'm sorry if I sound boastful, but I was really talented at making lenses and this led me to later make one of the first microscopes.

By the time I was about 40 years old, I began to use my microscope to study microbes, which are the smallest living things we know of.

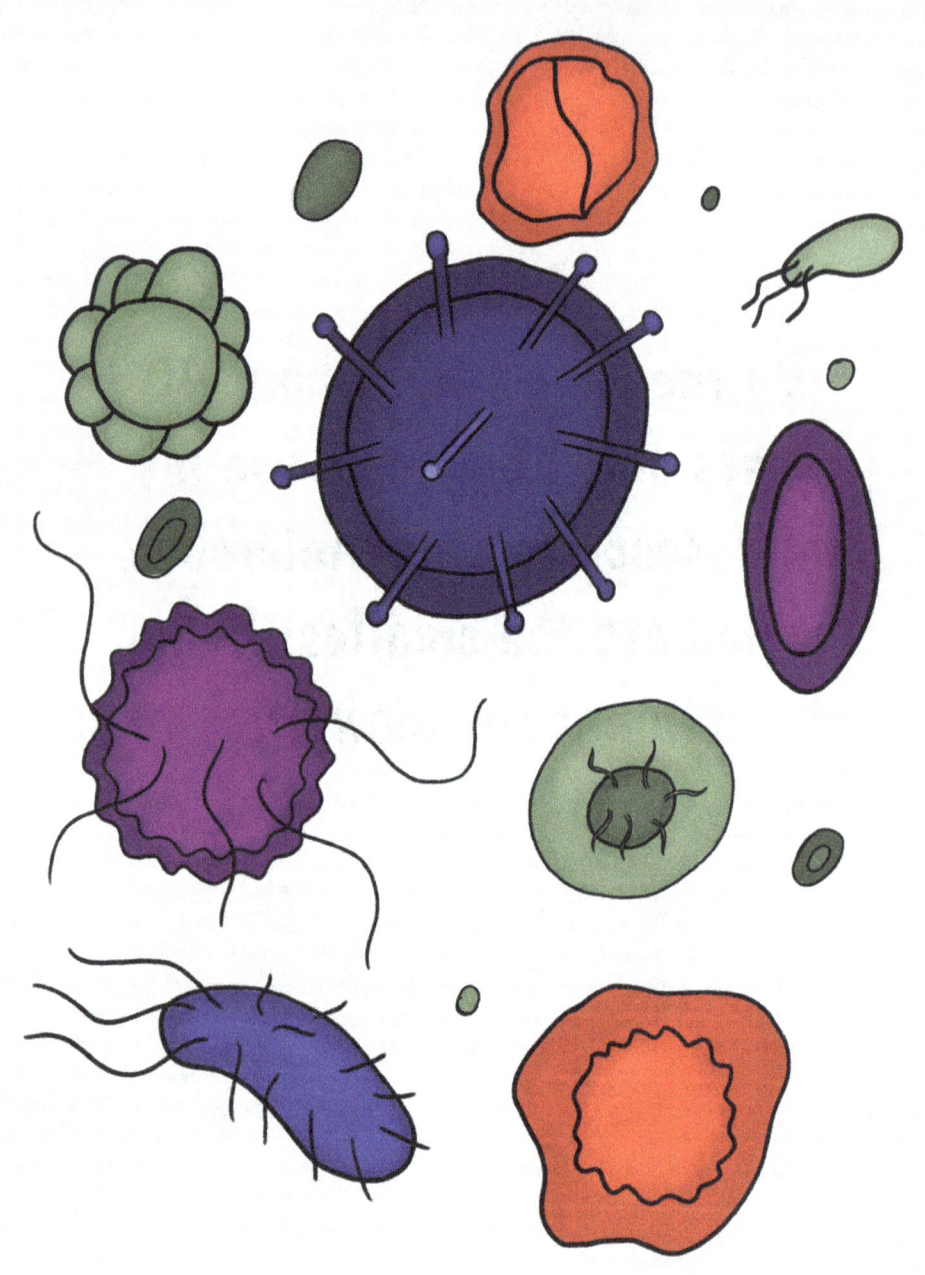

I called these life forms "tiny animals." Hey, what can I say? I call 'em as I see 'em. I was the first person to measure how small these creatures are.

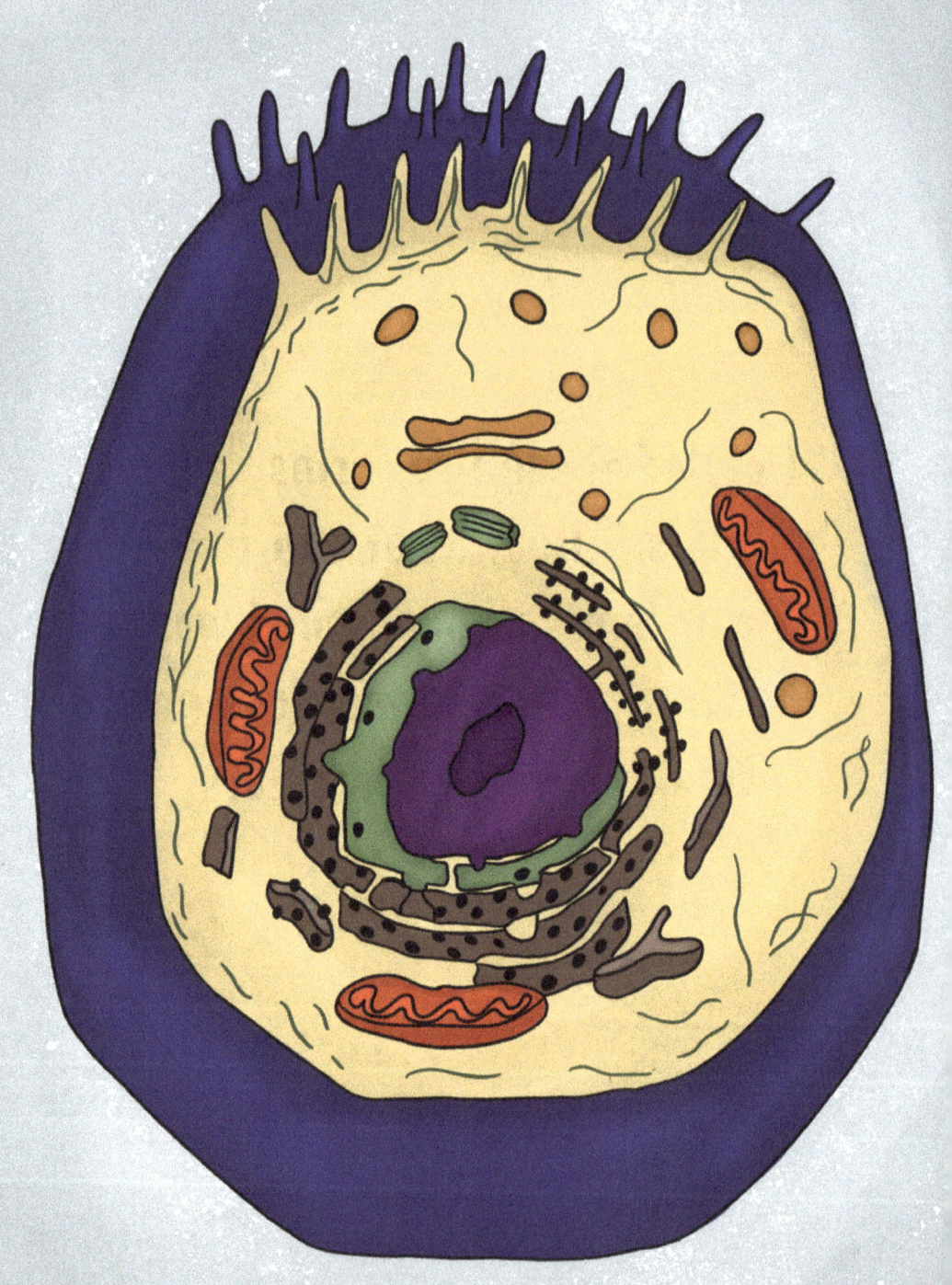

I didn't realize it at the time, but now it's well known many of these microbes are only made up of one cell.

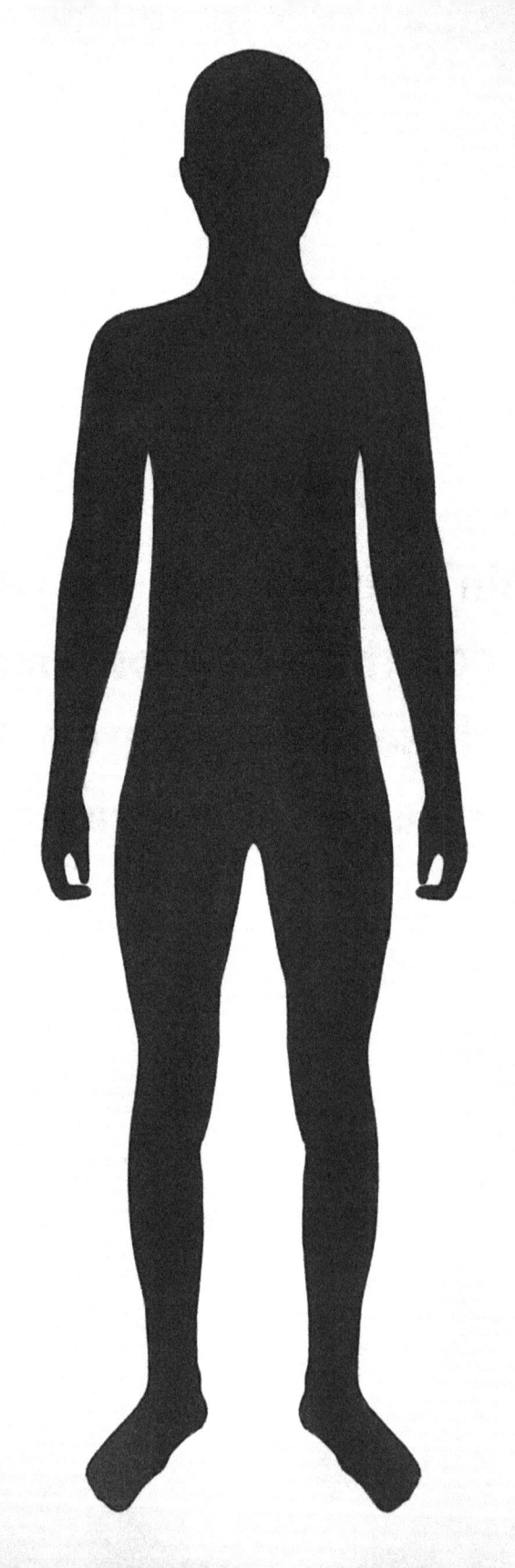

Just to compare, your body is made up of about 30 to 40 trillion cells. Whoa!

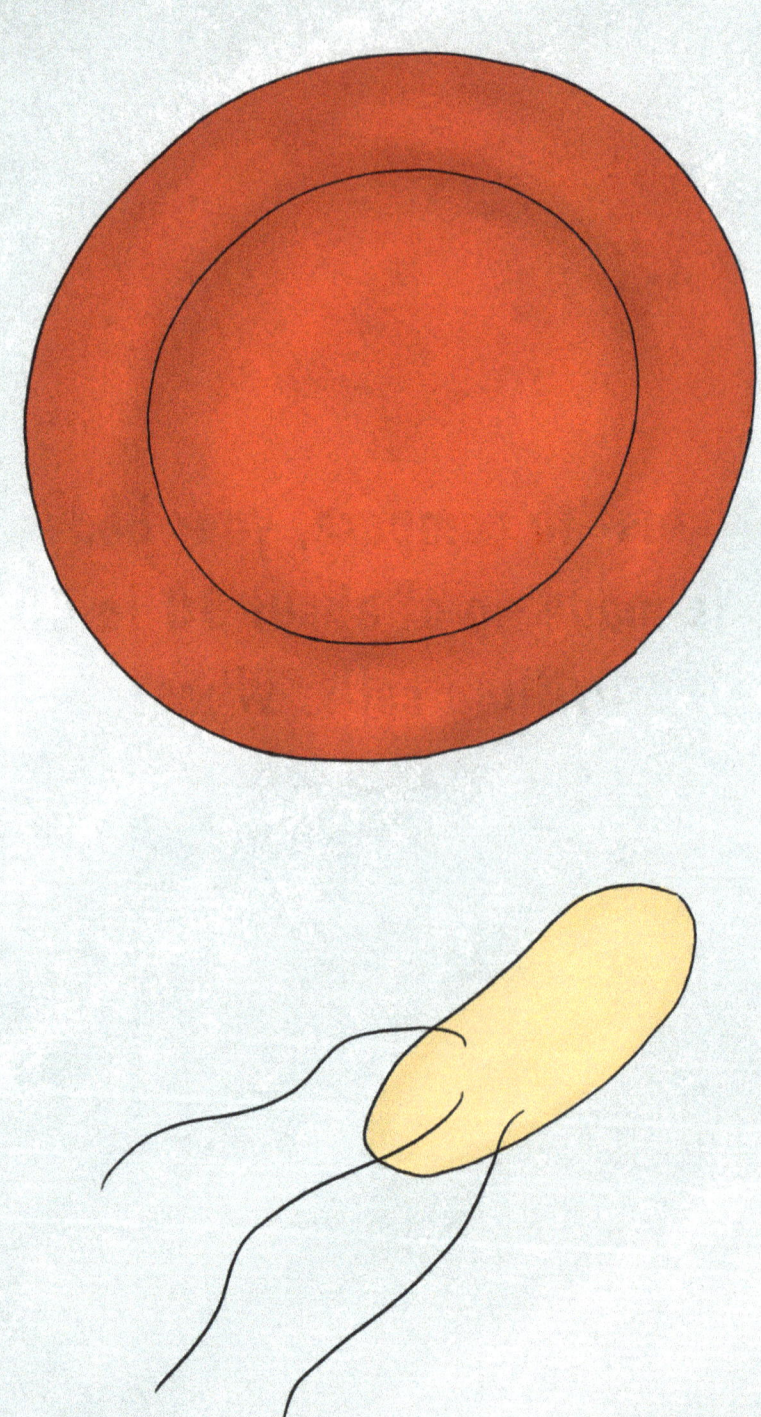

I later studied blood cells, and other things too small to see with our bare eyes.

I guess one could say I dedicated my life to seeing things no one even knew were there. Kind of like myself!

Hee hee. I crack myself up.

CPSIA information can be obtained
at www.ICGtesting.com
Printed in the USA
BVHW011712241121
622343BV00015B/18